C2 0000042 95411

KW-052-799

Get Writing!

Write that Letter

Che
to re

ww

ww

Shaun McCarthy

Heinemann
LIBRARY

www.heinemann.co.uk/library

Visit our website to find out more information about **Heinemann Library** books.

To order:

☎ Phone 44 (0) 1865 888066

▤ Send a fax to 44 (0) 1865 314091

▢ Visit the Heinemann Bookshop at www.heinemann.co.uk/library to browse our catalogue and order online.

First published in Great Britain by Heinemann Library, Halley Court, Jordan Hill, Oxford OX2 8EJ, part of Harcourt Education.

Heinemann is a registered trademark of Harcourt Education Ltd.

© Harcourt Education Ltd 2003
First published in paperback in 2004
The moral right of the proprietor has been asserted.

All rights reserved. No part of this publication may be reproduced, stored in a retrieval system, or transmitted in any form or by any means, electronic, mechanical, photocopying, recording, or otherwise, without either the prior written permission of the publishers or a licence permitting restricted copying in the United Kingdom issued by the Copyright Licensing Agency Ltd, 90 Tottenham Court Road, London W1T 4LP (www.cla.co.uk).

Editorial: Lucy Thunder and Helen Cox
Design: David Poole and Susan Clarke
Illustrations: George Hollingworth
Production: Séverine Ribierre
Origination: Dot Gradations
Printed in China by W K T

ISBN 0 431 15215 2 (hardback)
07 06 05 04 03
10 9 8 7 6 5 4 3 2 1

ISBN 0 431 15222 5 (paperback)
08 07 06 05 04
10 9 8 7 6 5 4 3 2 1

British Library Cataloguing in Publication Data

McCarthy, Shaun
  Write that Letter. – (Get Writing)
  808.6
A full catalogue record for this book is available from the British Library.

Cover design by David Poole, with illustrations by George Hollingworth

The publishers would like to thank Rachel Vickers for her assistance in the preparation of this book.

Every effort has been made to contact copyright holders of any material reproduced in this book. Any omissions will be rectified in subsequent printings if notice is given to the publishers.

Disclaimer

All the Internet addresses (URLs) given in this book were valid at the time of going to press. However, due to the dynamic nature of the Internet, some addresses may have changed, or sites may have ceased to exist since publication. While the author and publishers regret any inconvenience this may cause readers, no responsibility for any such changes can be accepted by either the author or the publishers.

BIRMINGHAM LIBRARIES	
C2 0000042 95411	
PETERS	Oct 2005
J 808.6	

SUTTON CHILDREN'S LIBRARY

Contents

Any words appearing in the text in bold, **like this**, are explained in the glossary.

Letters for life

Letters are very useful forms of writing – we write them throughout our lives. Many of our letters are chatty notes to friends, but it is important to learn how to write different types of letters. You need to know how to say what you want to say in the right **style**, and how to lay out your letters in the proper way. Then all you have to add is your imagination!

Dear Santa

Many of us write our first letter when we are very young – to Santa! This letter is a mix of friendly greeting and important information: a list of the presents you would like.

As you grow older, you go on to write 'thank you' letters to people; chatty ones to friends, and more **formal** ones to people you don't know so well.

Later on, you have to write more difficult letters. You might write to ask for information (to join a club) or complain about

Write a letter and surprise someone!

something. A letter of complaint can be tricky. You have to say what went wrong and what you would like to be done about it. Your letter has to sound sensible. Just being angry does not work!

When you are older still, you have to write letters of application for jobs or college places. You need to write these letters very carefully. You might also write letters to newspapers and magazines giving your **opinions** about something.

A letter checklist

There are several things you need to think about when you write a letter:

- who is going to read it?
- what do you want the letter to achieve?
- what image of yourself do you want the letter to create?
- how formal or **informal** does it have to be? (This means how friendly or how polite should the writing be.)
- how long should it be?
- how do you lay it out in the proper way?

@ Activity – a lifetime of letters

Think of all the people you have written to in your life. Write a list of as many of them as you can remember.

- friends who perhaps have moved away
- relatives
- pen pals
- brothers and sisters if they or you have been away
- Santa!

Try and remember why you wrote to these people and what type of letters they were. Did you write a letter, postcard or email? Jot this down beside the names.

Remember your reader

It is important that your letters sound right. Your **tone** and **style** must suit the purpose of the letter. Think about how you want the person receiving your letter to feel when they read it.

Setting the right tone

The tone of a letter is how you 'sound' to your reader. You might be clear and rather 'cold' sounding (**formal**), or you might be friendly and chatty (**informal**). The tone of a letter can be set by your choice of words.

- Formal – *I am sure you understand what I am saying.*
- Informal – *Know what I mean?*

Both these phrases mean the same thing, but the tone is different. For an informal letter you may use **slang**.

Write with style

Style is how to arrange your sentences for your reader. If you are being very formal, make sure each sentence is to the point and arrange your thoughts in an ordered way. If your letter is informal, you might include sentences that are more varied in length. You can sound more as though you are talking with your reader.

Think about who you are writing to

Here are some ideas to help you get the right tone and style in a letter – whether you are writing to a friend, or to a politician asking him or her to speak at your school.

Informal

For informal letters:

- Ask questions such as: *How is the new school?* Your friend can answer in their letter back to you.
- Include phrases that you would use in conversation, for example: *It was really funny, I couldn't stop laughing.*
- Use **rhetorical questions** (questions you ask then give the answer), especially when you are expressing an opinion or

telling a story. For example: *How can people say that tennis is boring? Of course it isn't,* or: *Guess what happened then?! Iqbal came in with a mask on!*

Formal

- Show that you are interested in how the reader will feel as he or she reads the letter. Use phrases such as: *I am sure that you are very busy but the school really would appreciate a visit by our local Member of Parliament.*
- Always be polite. If you want someone to do something, ask them nicely: *I would be very grateful if you could …*
- Think carefully about your choice of words. Don't be chatty or use slang. For example, it is better to say: *the school would be honoured to receive you* rather than: *the school would be totally over the moon to see you.*

@ Activity – sorting sentences

Look at the phrases in the box. They have been taken from different types of letter.

Sort them into two lists – one list for phrases that would be good for informal letters and one for formal letters.

Try describing your house to someone by writing one formal and one informal phrase or sentence.

You will find that most people of my age (I am 12) do not agree with what you say.

Then I tripped and fell in a puddle. It was so embarrassing!

My mum told me to tidy up my room – it's a right old mess.

Guess what I did yesterday?

I am wondering if you would be able to visit our school?

I am sure you will agree with me when I say that …

I don't care if I pass or fail the test. I mean, it's all boring, right?

Postcards

Postcards are a simple form of letter writing. You often write to tell your friends and family back home how a holiday is going. Even though your message may be short you should remember who you are writing to – choose the **tone** and **style** to suit your reader.

> Hi Sally,
> You'll never guess who I saw on the plane!

> Dear Mrs Jones,
> I have learnt many Spanish phrases during my week here.

First things first

You need to think carefully about how to say as much as you can in a few words. Plan the things you want to write by making a list. Arrange the list into order of importance and start with the first item. Then if you run out of space you will not miss out anything really important. Make sure your writing is neat if you are trying to squeeze a lot in.

Top tip

We often write postcards to friends. They know a lot about us — probably where we are and who we are with. Don't waste time explaining what they already know!

Wish you were here

If you are stuck over what to say to someone you don't know so well, think of one or two single events and describe them in detail to give the reader a picture of what happened. This is better than trying to list everything you have done.

> What a thunderstorm we had last night. The lightning lit up the sky and the thunder scared us to death. In the morning we almost didn't recognize the campsite

Activity – picture postcards

You are going on a school trip to sunny Spain. Unfortunately, your flight has been diverted to Iceland. The plane is stuck because of blizzards. The teachers are going crazy! It is cold because you only have clothes for Spain. Everyone is staying in a hotel where the food is raw fish and whale blubber steaks. But it is not all bad – you have made an Icelandic friend who works at the hotel and you are going on a sleigh ride together.

Write cards describing your trip to:
- your best friend
- your parents
- your class teacher who is back at school, who loves Spain
- your grandad, who is a serious old man.

Try to write no more than 80 words on each card. Match the way you describe events to the person you are writing to. Use your imagination to add extra details.

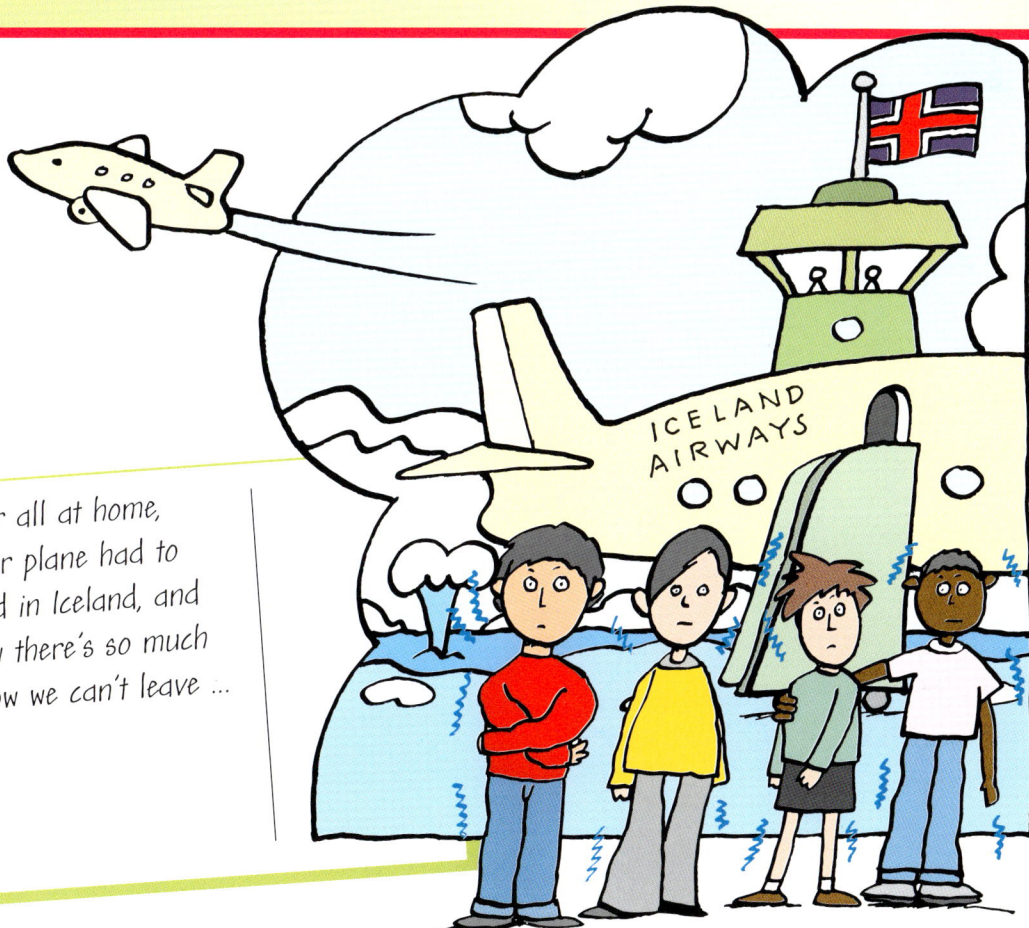

Dear all at home,
  Our plane had to land in Iceland, and now there's so much snow we can't leave ...

Make a good impression

People often glance quickly at a letter before they sit down and read it properly. A good, neat first impression is important. You do this with a tidy **layout**. If your letter is all cramped up on the page they might not bother to read it properly at all!

A friendly or informal letter

For an **informal** or friendly letter you put your address in the top right hand corner, with the date under that. Begin your letter with 'Dear ...', then write the main body of your letter underneath. Work from the left side of the page. See Figure 1.

SAM MILLS
21 Wood Street, Frampton
Tel: 0119 311 311
9th August 2010

Dear...

Best wishes
Sam

①

SAM MILLS
21 Wood Street, Frampton
Tel: 0119 311 311
9th August 2010

Computer Store
High St.
Plimpton

Dear...

Yours sincerely
Sam Mills

②

A formal or business letter

You lay out a business letter in the same way. However, for this sort of letter you put the name and address of the person you are writing to on the left before you begin the letter itself. See Figure 2. You can add your phone number and email address at the bottom of your address if you want.

Signing off

There are different ways to finish, or sign off, a letter:

- If you know the name of the person you are writing to, and have started the letter *Dear Mr Smith*, for example, end the letter with *Yours sincerely*.
- If you have started the letter *Dear Sir or Madam*, end with *Yours faithfully*.
- If you are writing to a friend you can replace *Yours sincerely*, or *Yours faithfully*, with anything you like!
- If you have a signature that is hard to read, print your name under it at the end of the letter.

Samuel

12 Merryvale Avenue,
Fernwood,
Yorkshire
SB7 2AE

25th October 2020

Dear Jim,

    I am having a fancy dress party on 20th November. I hope you can come. It starts at 6 p.m. and finishes at 8.30.

    I am dressing as Spider Man and my little sister wants to be a fairy. My mum is having to make wings for her and she is going crazy! My dad is threatening to dress up as Batman. Luckily, I don't think he'll find an outfit to fit him.

    I hope to hear from you soon.

Love

Anita

@ Activity – party time

Look at the letter above. Imagine you have also been invited to Anita's fancy dress party. You need to hire an outfit for the party.

Write a business letter to a mail-order fancy dress company asking them if the outfit you want is available and how much it would cost.

Write an informal letter to a friend and tell them what happened at the party. Did Anita's dad dress up as Batman? What did her naughty little sister get up to?

Pay lots of attention to how you lay your letters out.

Word processing your letters

If you have a computer at home or at school you can use it for writing letters. Experiment with different **fonts** and colours. Once you are happy with your design, you can keep it on the computer as a **template** to use for all your letter writing.

What font?

Your computer may have a large number of fonts to choose from. You could decide on one and stick to it or you may want to change the font to suit your letter. For example, if you are inviting friends to watch a scary movie you could use a font of 'melting writing'. For a serious letter, choose a clear, neat font like the example on the left.

I would like to apply …

Come round to my house on Saturday and we can watch a scary movie.

Computer know-how

Use these points to make your word processed letters as good as possible:

- Make sure your type size is not set too small or too big.
- Use the tab key to line up your blocks of type.
- Use the electronic spellchecker to check your spelling and grammar.
- If you have 'print preview' on your computer, check the position of your letter on the page before you print.
- Print out two copies if you are writing a **formal** or business letter so you can keep one as a record.

Business letters

Word processed letters can look more formal than handwritten ones. This makes word processing ideal for business letters.

Some business letters need you to quote a reference number. This is so your letter can be filed or passed to the right person. You put this reference number on the left, under the address of the person you are sending your letter to. The letter below shows a word processed letter set out in the correct way.

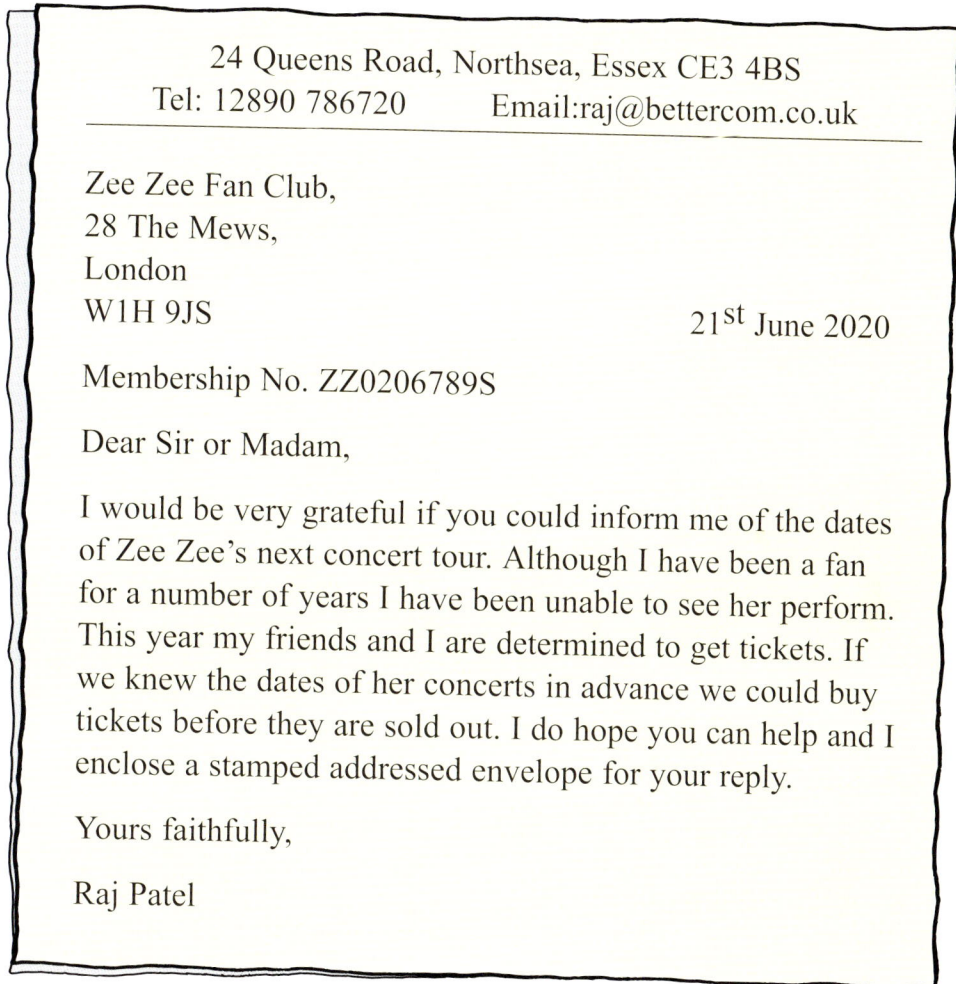

24 Queens Road, Northsea, Essex CE3 4BS
Tel: 12890 786720   Email:raj@bettercom.co.uk

Zee Zee Fan Club,
28 The Mews,
London
W1H 9JS

21st June 2020

Membership No. ZZ0206789S

Dear Sir or Madam,

I would be very grateful if you could inform me of the dates of Zee Zee's next concert tour. Although I have been a fan for a number of years I have been unable to see her perform. This year my friends and I are determined to get tickets. If we knew the dates of her concerts in advance we could buy tickets before they are sold out. I do hope you can help and I enclose a stamped addressed envelope for your reply.

Yours faithfully,

Raj Patel

Activity – be creative

Try making your own letter template using a computer. You could print your address along the top in one line, or even up the side. All sorts of designs are possible. You may wish to have one template for formal letters and another one for friendly letters.

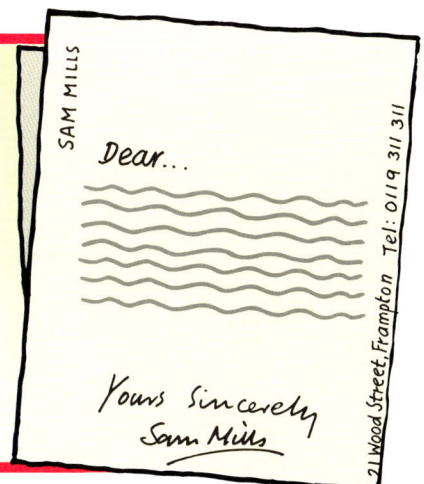

SAM MILLS

Dear...

Yours sincerely
Sam Mills

21 Wood Street, Frampton Tel: 0119 311 311

Lively letters

Describing things that happen can be an interesting part of many different sorts of letters. We often want to tell friends what we have been doing. Even in a business letter you sometimes describe events. For example, if you are complaining about a journey you will need to describe what went wrong.

Order, order!

Many descriptions are like little stories with a beginning, middle and an end. Make sure you get the order of events right. It will make a letter easier and more entertaining to read. If you are complaining about a journey, the reader will need to be clear about what happened, and when.

Top tip

Before you start writing your letter, make a list of the events you want to include. Put them in the correct order. This will make sure you don't forget anything.

Choosing the details

You need to think about what your reader would like to know from your letter. You cannot usually describe everything, so pick

the things you think will interest them or be useful. For example, a pen pal may want to know about a typical day at your school. You could describe some of the main things that happen in the day, from beginning to end. Add in some personal and funny little details too. If your pen pal is coming to stay for a whole term, then make your letter less jokey. You will need to describe more practical details, such as what time lessons start and finish.

Mind your language

When describing events to a friend, try and make your description as vivid as possible. Think carefully about the words you choose. For example, rather than saying: *Mr Clarke was angry*, you could describe him as: *red with anger*. Choose words that will show your feelings about events, for example: *I was really upset*. In a **formal** letter you might say: *I was deeply concerned ....*

@ Activity – describe a day

Imagine you have been on a school outing like the one in the picture. Write a letter to a friend describing it. Put the phrases below in the correct order and use them to help you with your letter.

- We stumbled off the bus exhausted.
- We had to eat breakfast while running for the bus.
- The best thing was the water slide.
- You should have seen Sally dive. She's brilliant.
- Sanjay's ice cream got stuck in his hair!
- Miss Herbert fell in the pool – we couldn't stop laughing.
- Then I lost my clothes!
- Tom turned green and the bus had to stop for him!

Having your say

Sometimes we feel so strongly about something that we want to write a letter stating our views. It might be to a single person or to an organization – for example, to a television company about a programme. You might write an **open letter** to a newspaper to be printed on its letters page. A letter like this can be a form of **protest**.

Get the message across

Convince your reader that your point of view is best by:

- planning your letter carefully before you start. Make a list of points to include, like the plan here.
- making your points quickly and clearly
- keeping your letter short to grab the reader's attention.

Letter plan

The new motorway by the village of Icklefield.

Will destroy an area of forest

- chopping down trees that have been there for centuries
- birds and animals will have their habitat destroyed
- tourist industry of the area will be damaged as visitors will no longer come to walk in the forest

Will increase number of cars and lorries

- causes pollution with exhaust fumes
- very noisy
- fast traffic will make the village roads dangerous

Top tip

A bullet point list is a good way of saving words in your letter. Have a paragraph before the list saying what you are writing about and how you feel about the subject. Then give your list of points to support your views.

Introducing the topic

Decide if you need to give your reader any background information. If fox hunting has been in the news in your area, for example, readers will probably know what you are writing about. However, if you are writing about something new, add a brief introduction to explain it to your reader, like this:

Last summer, plans were drawn up for a new road that will cut through the forests of Icklefield ...

Activity – curfew time

In some areas where there is a lot of crime on the streets, the local council is introducing **curfews** for young people. A curfew is a time by which people of a certain age have to be inside. If they are out after this time, they can be stopped by the police and taken home.

Some people who live in these areas say the curfew is a good plan. It stops gangs of youths causing trouble at night. Others say it stops young people from seeing their friends, and that it is not just young people (certainly not all young people) who cause trouble.

Imagine a curfew is being planned for your area. Everyone up to the age of fifteen has to be indoors by 9p.m. Write a letter about it to your local radio station, giving your view.

*And now your letters.
Our debate about curfews for young people has brought dozens of letters for and against.
Mrs Trevis of North Wales says ...*

Writing instructions

You can use letters to send instructions to people. Make sure your instructions are clear and properly ordered.

- Use short sentences. Try not to have more than one instruction per sentence. Your instructions should be a series of steps. For example:

  Turn right at the roundabout. Now keep going straight.

- Think about how much information to give. If you are giving route directions to someone who knows the area, keep them simple. Too much information can be as confusing as too little.
- Set out your instructions clearly on the page. You can do this with a numbered list, bullet points or simply write each stage on a separate line.
- Read your instructions through and see if you can follow them yourself.

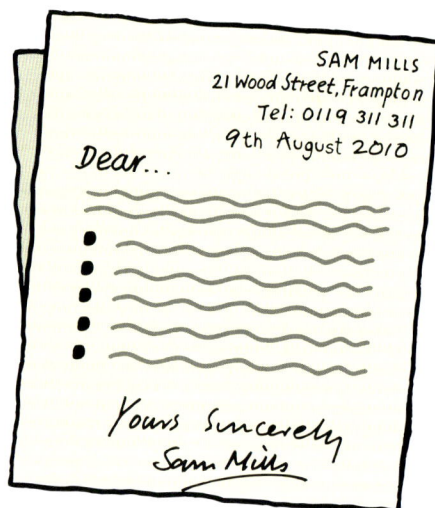

SAM MILLS
21 Wood Street, Frampton
Tel: 0119 311 311
9th August 2010

Dear...

Yours sincerely
Sam Mills

Activity – map reading

Look carefully at the map opposite. It shows your house, the railway station, roads and main features of the town where you live.

Write a letter to your uncle and aunt giving instructions on how to get to your new house. Your visitors do not know yet if they are travelling by car or by train. You have to give them two sets of directions: one from the M32 by car and the other from the train station on foot. They get lost easily so make your instructions very clear.

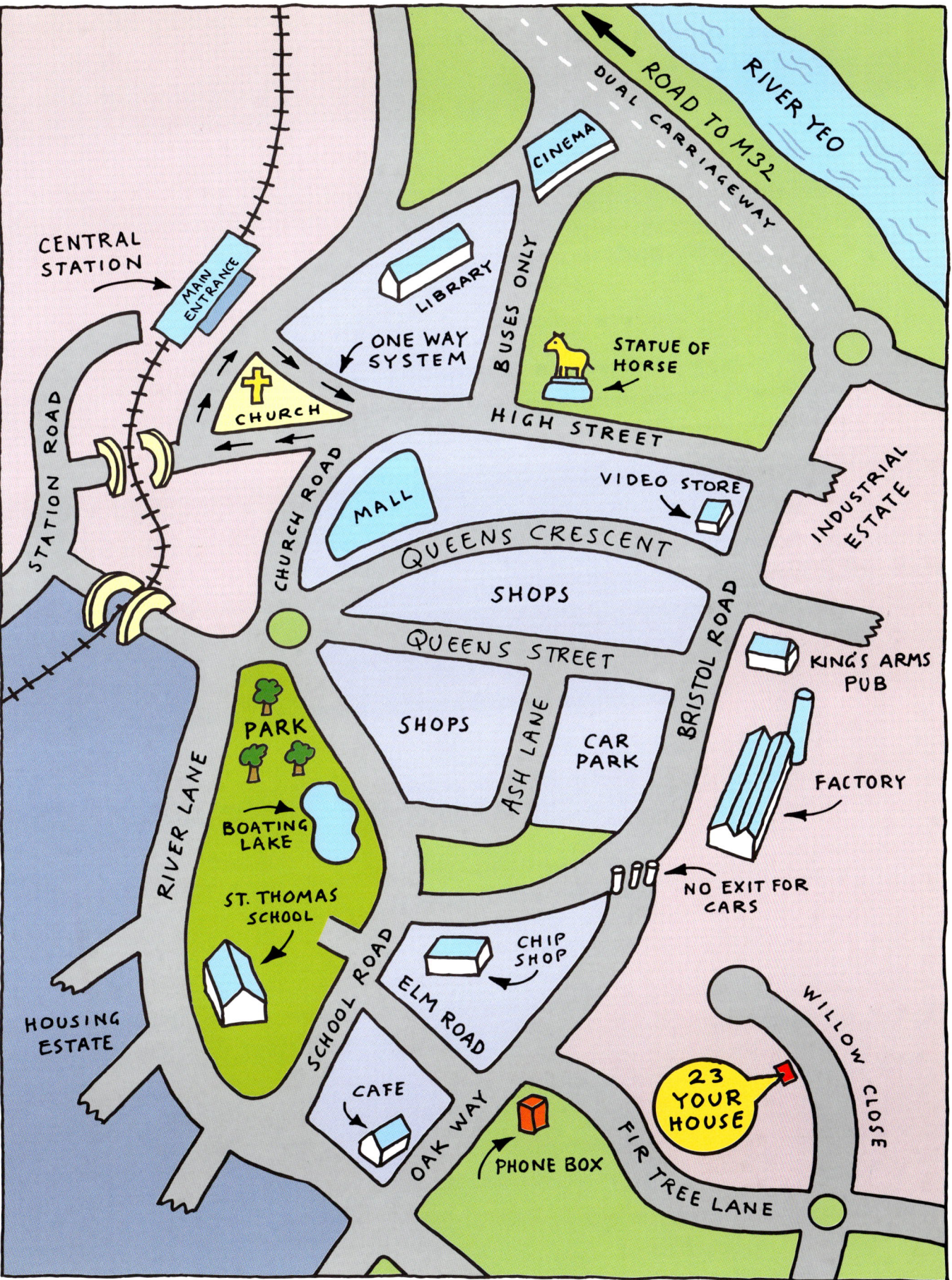

CENTRAL STATION

MAIN ENTRANCE

CINEMA

ROAD TO M32

DUAL CARRIAGEWAY

RIVER YEO

LIBRARY

ONE WAY SYSTEM

BUSES ONLY

STATUE OF HORSE

CHURCH

HIGH STREET

STATION ROAD

CHURCH ROAD

MALL

QUEENS CRESCENT

SHOPS

VIDEO STORE

INDUSTRIAL ESTATE

QUEENS STREET

SHOPS

ASH LANE

CAR PARK

KING'S ARMS PUB

BRISTOL ROAD

FACTORY

RIVER LANE

PARK

BOATING LAKE

ST. THOMAS SCHOOL

NO EXIT FOR CARS

HOUSING ESTATE

SCHOOL ROAD

ELM ROAD

CHIP SHOP

WILLOW CLOSE

CAFE

OAK WAY

PHONE BOX

23 YOUR HOUSE

FIR TREE LANE

I want to complain

When something we have recently bought breaks or an offer does not match up to the advert, we can feel cheated and angry. We want to write a letter of complaint to tell the company how we feel and to get things sorted out. So how do you make sure your letter has the right effect?

Don't get angry

It is tempting to write an angry letter, but it will not help. Your aim is to get something replaced or repaired, or to get your money back. To do this:

- explain clearly what went wrong
- say how this made you feel
- explain what you want done.

Top tip

Make sure what you are asking for is reasonable. You will get what you want much more quickly than someone who sends a letter demanding all sorts of impossible things!

My hamster is unhappy

Imagine you bought a special 'activity cage' for your pet hamster, but soon after it fell to bits. The letter of complaint on page 21 shows the sort of letter you could write. The numbers on the list match those next to the letter:

1 Explain in a few lines why you are writing.
2 Describe what you bought, and why you chose it.
3 Say what went wrong. If several things went wrong, list them in order.
4 Say what you want the company to do about it.
5 Explain what you will do if the company doesn't do what you suggest.

15 Cross St
London
E6 9NE

Pets U Like
9 Marsh St
Marsden
Surrey

20th January 2020

Dear Sir or Madam,

1 – 2 — I saw an advert for your 'hamster home' activity. I bought the luxury edition and put it together by following your instructions. I expected it to provide a safe and fun-filled cage for my pet.

3 — Within days, parts of the cage started falling apart. The tubes that make up his runs became unclipped. The nest-part fell off. Then the main outside walls came apart at the corners and he escaped. It was very worrying and annoying.

4 — I think the design of the cage is wrong and the plastic parts will always come apart. I would therefore like a refund. The **guarantee** offers money back if the cage does not work. I can send the cage back to you if you want to see that it is broken.

5 — I am sure you will give me a refund, but if you do not, I feel I should write to *Hamster Weekly* to warn other owners of the problems of your product.

Yours faithfully,

Activity – it pays to complain

Imagine you have just bought a CD of the latest chart-topping band. The cover and the CD label are right, but the music on the CD is German opera. The CD you wanted has now sold out, but you want the shop to take the opera back and find a copy of the band's CD. You would also like a free poster of the band to make up for your disappointment.

Write a letter of complaint to the shop. Use your imagination to bring some extra details into your letter.

I would like to apply

You write letters of application when you apply for a job or want to join a club. They are probably the most important letters you will ever write. You really want to get into that team, be accepted at that college, get that job! In a letter of application, you have to say some things that you know people want to hear, while still being truthful about yourself.

What you have to offer

Give sensible suggestions about why you would be good in a club or doing a job. Back up what you say with facts about your skills and **experience**. Match your skills to the post you are applying for. For example, if you are applying to join a local sports club, tell them about the football or hockey you play at school, not the computer games you play in your room!

Top tip

With all your letters, make a plan before you start. List what you want to say in your letter and tick off each item as you write it in. Remember to put the important details first.

Order it

Your letter of application should have the following points – in this order:

- detail of what you are applying for
    I would like to apply for the post of …
- why you want to apply
    I have always been an enthusiastic hockey player and would welcome the chance to become secretary of the club.
- a list of the experience that is useful for your application. Write these in order of importance.

In my previous school I was secretary of the nature club. I had to keep a record of all our meetings. I was also responsible for looking after the nature collection.

- description of the **skills** you have that you think will be needed for the place or job

    I am very organized. I also get on well with other people.

- a polite ending to your letter

    I do hope that you will consider my application.

    I look forward to hearing from you.

Why do I want to work at Burger Swamp? I need the money! Can't say that … How about 'I'd enjoy working hard in a lively place with other young people'?

Activity – join a team

Think of a sport you enjoy playing. Imagine you want to join the best local team in your area.

Write a letter of application, saying exactly why you would be a good new team member. List things about yourself that would make you look good, for example: you are reliable and would always turn up for training.

Emails

Emails can be a great way of staying in touch with friends!
Emails are replacing many letters that people used to send
through the post.

Here are some of the advantages of using email:
- Emails are sent and received immediately.
- You can type a quick reply to an email that you receive, and
  send it straight back by clicking on 'reply'.
- All emails you send or receive are instantly filed in your
  computer, so you have a copy of them.
- You can type several addresses into an email and send it to
  several people at once.
- You can attach **documents** or video clips to the email.

Email chat

People often write emails quickly. A lot of the time they are
informal. They can sound a bit like a telephone conversation
like this example here:

> Hi Jo
> Did you see that band last night on the TV – weren't they cool?
> Jess
>
> Yeah, especially that guitarist!!!
> Jo

Don't get careless

Don't be too careless when typing emails. You
should always run the electronic spellchecker to check the
spelling and grammar before you send it. An email still needs to
give the right impression to the person who receives it.

Try to keep your **style** clear and precise, just like you would
for a letter written on paper. Remember to suit your **tone** to
your reader.

Top tip

In emails to friends you can add an emoticon or smiley. This is a symbol which looks like a face and shows how you are feeling. For example :) for happy, or this :(for sad.

Getting attached

Business emails often have 'attachments' added to them. These are usually documents (files) from the word processing part of the computer added to the email. Sending a letter as an attachment can be more **formal**. For example, you might write a formal letter of application and send it as an attachment.

Activity – email fun

Write an email to a friend about your favourite band or pop star. Describe who they are and why you like them. Make sure that what you write is as a clear and neat as a letter written on paper. You might even add in a smiley or two!

You could also send pictures of the band or star to your friend as an attachment to your email.

Two points of view

You can now use the letter writing skills you have practised to write different types of letters. Remember to choose the right **layout** and **style** for each letter.

Holiday from hell

Three friends booked a five-day horse-riding course during the school holidays. However, the course did not match up to what the stable advertised. These were the basic problems:

- the stable yard was always full of mud and horse manure
- the horses were always dirty
- to get to the fields meant taking the horses over a busy road
- the instructor lost her temper easily and shouted
- the horses were not all well-trained — some of them bit
- the food was horrible
- there was nowhere to have a shower and change at the end of the day.

@ Activity – polite complaint

Imagine you were one of the friends on the course.

Write a letter of complaint to the stable. Use your imagination to add any other details you like. Be polite but determined. You want some of your money back, and you also want an apology from the riding instructor who was rude when you complained.

Activity – horseplay

Now imagine that you are another of the friends. Write a letter to a pen pal, telling them what you have been doing. Go over the problems you and your friends had, but this time use a style that is less serious. Turn things you complained about into stories. Try to make some of them funny. Mention some details that you thought it best not to mention in your letter of complaint such as:

- you and your friends did not help clean the yard, and threw hay at each other instead
- the horses were dirty because your group did not groom (brush and clean) them properly, even though grooming was part of the course
- you visited the village shop everyday and had midnight feasts.

Maybe it seems you had quite a fun time after all!

Top tip

You can sign off a friendly letter in any way you choose. It is a good way of showing friendship or affection to the person you are writing to. Think of different ways to end your **informal** letters, such as 'Take care', 'Bye for now', 'Love'.

How have I done?

When you have finished a letter, read it through carefully. Use the checklists below to answer the question 'was this the best letter I could have written?'

Content

- Have you included all the important and necessary points in your letter?
- Are all the points in the right order (very important if you are writing instructions or applying for a job)?
- Have you checked your spelling, grammar and punctuation?

Tone and style

- Have you thought about who will be reading your letter?
- Does your **style** of writing match the type of letter?
- Is the **tone** of your letter right? Have you made sure it is not too chatty or 'jokey' for a business letter?

Are you trying to be funny?

Layout

- Is your letter neatly and clearly laid out?
- Have you included your address, the address of the person you are sending the letter to (if it is a **formal** letter) and the date?
- Have you signed off correctly?

A letter about Hamlet

You can write letters about anything – even Shakespeare's great play *Hamlet!* It takes place in a Danish castle. Claudius has murdered Hamlet's father, who was king of Denmark. Claudius then marries Hamlet's mother, Gertrude, and becomes king. Only Hamlet knows about the murder and he hates Claudius.

In the last part of the play Hamlet has a sporting sword fight using blunted swords with Laertes, a young man who hates Hamlet. Hamlet does not know that Laertes' sword is both sharp and poisoned. Both Claudius and Laertes want Hamlet dead. People are watching and cheering – they think the fight is for fun. When Hamlet becomes wounded, the fighting turns serious. Gertrude drinks to Hamlet's success, but the drink is poisoned and she dies. Hamlet kills Laertes and Claudius, but dies from his poisoned wound. A Norwegian general called Fortinbras arrives at the castle. He learns that he will become king of Denmark.

@ Activity – writing home about Hamlet

Imagine you are an English traveller visiting the court, to see the king on business. You watch the whole scene.

Keeping the checklists in mind, write a letter home describing what you saw. Imagine the castle, the young men fighting with swords and the king, Claudius, looking on. You are writing to your best friend so the letter can be quite **informal**. Try to cover all the main points of the story.

Dear Jane,
I've been at the court of the Danish king for just two days and you'll never believe what I am about to tell you ...

Glossary

curfew law stating that people must stay indoors between certain hours of the evening or night

document written piece of information

experience skills and knowledge that a person has developed and learnt

font style of letters that are a particular shape. A computer usually has lots you can choose from. Times New Roman and Arial are the most well known.

formal style of writing that is polite and business-like

guarantee formal promise that something is made to good standards. For example, a kettle may be guaranteed for a year in case it breaks down during that time.

informal style of writing that is quite chatty and relaxed

layout how a letter looks on a page

open letter letter sent to a magazine or newspaper for publication. It is not written to be read by one person, but by all the readers of the magazine or newspaper.

opinion personal feelings on a subject

protest show disagreement with something

rhetorical question question that is asked but does not need an answer, or an answer is immediately provided. For example, *What makes you say that? I think you are wrong.*

slang popular words or phrases that are spoken or written in an informal way

style arrangement of words and sentences in a particular manner

template layout or design that can be used again and again

tone how a letter sounds. For example, friendly or business-like.

Find out more

More books to read

Here are some books with letters in that you might enjoy:

Chain Letter (The Babysitters Club), Anne M. Martin (Scholastic, 1993).
Letters written to friends right across the USA telling their secrets.

P.S. Longer Letter Later, Paula Danziger and Anne M. Martin (Hodder Children's Books, 1999).
Two friends write letters to each other when one of them moves away.

Snail Mail No More, Paula Danziger and Anne M. Martin (Hodder Children's Books, 1999).
The two best friends are still in touch but now they write to each other by email!

Loathsome Letter Writing Pack, Martin Brown (Scholastic Hippo, 1997).
This letter-writing pack contains 20 sheets of writing paper, 12 envelopes and some stickers. Get writing!

Websites

Here are some websites which might help you with your letter writing:

http://www.learn.co.uk/default.asp?WC1=Unit&WCU=489
Winner of the Best Education Site 2001, the above address will lead you straight to more advice on letter-writing.

http://www.teachingideas.co.uk/english/
Gives further advice on letter-writing.

Index